Science • ENVIRONMENTAL SCIENCE

Reading Level: **5** Interest Level: **4–6**

Green Tech

Aspiring engineers likely know they face a future where they have their work cut out for them with global issues such as climate change and pollution. However, this exciting set introduces readers to the variety of technological advancements that are already tackling these massive problems. Just one example: nanotechnology that can break down microplastics! Relevant topics covered include safe drinking water, eco-friendly living, protecting wildlife, and climate crisis solutions.

- Explanatory text describes environmental problems and innovative technological solutions
- A mix of engaging illustrations and eye-catching full-color photos are on every dynamically designed spread
- Fascinating fact boxes expand on key ideas of environmental issues and the technology that is addressing them
- Diagrams demonstrate natural processes, including the water cycle
- Provides a glossary to enhance vocabulary skills and a list of resources for further information about technological solutions to environmental problems

Actual Type Size

School & Library Price reflects 25% off the List Price

		S&L
Library-bound Book		$20.45
eBook		$20.45
4-Book Print Set		$81.80 978-1-5383-8743-6

TITLE	DEWEY	GRL	ATOS	©
① **Clean and Safe Water** Katie Dicker • 978-1-7253-3859-3 eBook: 978-1-7253-3860-9		Q	PENDING	©2023 RR13312 ①
② **Eco-friendly Living** Katie Dicker • 978-1-7253-3863-0 eBook: 978-1-7253-3864-7		Q	PENDING	©2023 RR13313 ②
③ **Protecting Nature and Wildlife** Alice Harman • 978-1-7253-3867-8 eBook: 978-1-7253-3868-5		Q	PENDING	©2023 RR13314 ③
④ **Solving the Climate Crisis** Alice Harman • 978-1-7253-3871-5 eBook: 978-1-7253-3872-2		Q	PENDING	©2023 RR13315 ④

Reading Level: **5**   Interest Level: **4–6**

8 1/2" x 11" • Library Binding • 32 pp. • Full-Color Photographs • "Did You Know?" Fun Fact Boxes • Diagrams • Fact Boxes • Further Information Section • Glossary • Index • Sidebars

Clean and Safe Water

CLEAN AND SAFE WATER

KATIE DICKER

PowerKiDS press
New York

Published in 2023 by The Rosen Publishing Group, Inc.
29 East 21st Street, New York, NY 10010

Copyright © 2021 Wayland, a division of Hachette Children's Group

All rights reserved. No part of this book may be reproduced in any form without permission in writing from the publisher, except by a reviewer.

Editor: Katie Dicker
Designer: Clare Nicholas
Series Designer: Rocket Design (East Anglia) Ltd
Consultant: Dr Sharon George

Cataloging-in-Publication Data
Names: Dicker, Katie.
Title: Clean and safe water / Katie Dicker.
Description: New York : Powerkids Press, 2023. | Series: Green tech | Includes glossary and index.
Identifiers: ISBN 9781725338579 (pbk.) | ISBN 9781725338593 (library bound) | ISBN 9781725338586 (6pack) | ISBN 9781725338609 (ebook)
Subjects: LCSH: Water-supply--Juvenile literature. | Water quality--Juvenile literature. | Water quality management--Juvenile literature.
Classification: LCC TD348.D565 2023 | DDC 363.6'1--dc23

Picture acknowledgements:
Alamy: Ann and Steve Toon / Alamy Stock Photo 9tr; Courtesy of Michael Hoffmann/Caltech 28; Getty: Yauhen44 3t and 29tr, Bullet_Chained 4t, hadynyah 4b. intararit 10, 16–17, 24t, 31tr, ONYXprj 18, Goddard_Photography 21t, Moorefam 23t, Dorling Kindersley 25b, lucato 27b, Trifonenko 29bl; Science Photo Library: MIKKEL JUUL JENSEN 21b; Shutterstock: ananaline cover tl and title tl, Paranyu cover tr and title tr, Macrovector cover ml, Nanashiro cover m and title bl, Natali Snailcat cover m and title bl, Amanita Silvicora cover mr, 22t, 23b and 32, GraphicsRF.com cover bl and title br, Macrovector cover bm, Golden Sikorka cover br, DRogatnev 2, Crystal Eye Studio 3b and 14, intararit 5t, SVPanteon 5bl, HappyPictures 5bm, Fir4ik 5br, Good_Stock 6, Unitone Vector 7t, Arisa_J 8t, pixinoo 8b, Erin Donalson 9mr, ordinary man 9br, Jurasam 9b, Hennadii H 11t and 30–31, LINE ICONS 11b, Nic Keller 12t, Scharfsinn 12b, CLUSTERX 13t, tele52 13b, Damsea 15b, Pro_Vector 16t, paramouse 19t, Pete Niesen 19b, Vectorpocket 20t, Pogorelova Olga 20b, dani daniar 22b, romeovip_md 25mr, Mironova Iuliia 26t, Sudowoodo 26m, Eva Speshneva 26b, Yuri Schmidt 26bl, DwaFotografy 26br, CRS PHOTO 27t, Arcady 29br; © Tarmac Trading Limited 24b; The Ocean and Climate Platform reference for 18; The Seabin Project reference for 17; UNEP Young Champions of the Earth 7b.

All design elements from Shutterstock or drawn by designer.

Manufactured in the United States of America

CPSIA Compliance Information: Batch #CSPK23. For further information contact Rosen Publishing, New York, New York at 1-800-237-9932.

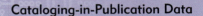
Find us on

CONTENTS

WHY IS CLEAN WATER IMPORTANT?	4
WATER PURIFICATION	6
HARVESTING WATER	8
SMART CONTROLLERS	10
FRESHWATER POLLUTION	12
SALTWATER DESALINATION	14
PLASTIC DEBRIS	16
OCEAN ACIDIFICATION	18
OIL SPILLS	20
LIVING SHORELINES	22
URBAN SOLUTIONS	24
SAVING WATER	26
BASIC SANITATION	28
GLOSSARY	30
FURTHER INFORMATION	31
INDEX	32

WHY IS CLEAN WATER IMPORTANT?

Earth is the only planet in our solar system to have a vast quantity of liquid water to sustain life. Yet, although water covers 71 percent of Earth's surface, less than 3 percent of this is fresh (not salty). Access to clean water is vital for the survival of plants, people and animals.

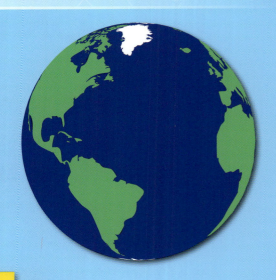

LIMITED ACCESS

Nearly 70 percent of Earth's fresh water is found in glaciers (which are mostly inaccessible). With such limited supplies, we need to clean more of the water we can reach. Research shows that 10 percent of the world's population don't have access to clean water, which has an impact on their daily lives. Drinking dirty water (or eating with dirty hands) can spread serious diseases. Walking miles each day to collect water, or falling sick from water-borne diseases, can affect work and educational opportunities. With limited water supplies, it's harder to grow food too.

These women are collecting water in the Thar Desert in India. Every day, 200 million working hours are lost by women collecting water for their families.

GROWING PROBLEM

In recent years, climate change has affected our freshwater supplies. The glacial meltwater that some people rely on is disappearing. Flooding, caused by an increase in rainfall, brings a risk of contamination. Heavy rains can cause water treatment facilities and sewage systems to overflow, and rising sea levels add salt to our water supplies. Evaporation caused by droughts can also lower water levels in lakes and rivers, increasing the concentration of pollutants.

Flood waters can carry 1,000 times the usual number of disease-causing bacteria, as well as pesticides, dissolved metals and other pollutants.

THE POWER OF TECH

There are lots of things we can do to reduce our water use and reuse our water supplies (see pages 26–27). But as our demand for water grows and Earth's population increases, time isn't on our side. Thankfully, some amazing technology is helping to speed up the process. Green tech has provided ways to harvest and purify more water, to find leaks in our water systems, and to help clean up pollution, so we can use this precious resource as efficiently as possible.

HOW MUCH WATER?

If a bucket contained all the world's water, about a teacup of this would be fresh water, and only a teaspoon would be accessible. Of this accessible fresh water, 70 percent is used for agriculture, 20 percent for industry and 10 percent for household use.

WATER PURIFICATION

With increasing demands for water and a changing climate, the quantity and quality of our water supplies are under threat. One of the simplest ways to increase access to clean and safe water is to purify the water sources we have.

FINDING SOLUTIONS

In richer countries, wastewater treatment facilities purify water supplies (see page 13). Lack of clean water mainly affects poorer countries, so solutions need to be affordable and easy to maintain. Filtering water can be slow and impractical, and using disinfectants, such as chlorine, adds a taste (and needs just the right amount, as too much can be toxic). Thankfully scientists have come up with some ingenious solutions.

Scientists predict that by 2040, the effects of climate change will cause one in four children worldwide to have limited access to water.

TINY PARTICLES

Nanotechnology uses nanoparticles – tiny particles that are hundreds of times smaller than the width of a human hair. Magnetic nanoparticles release ions (electrically charged particles) that attract lead and copper contaminants and stop the growth of some bacteria. The nanoparticles can then be removed by magnets. Scientists have also found that gold nanoparticles absorb sunlight, which heats the water's surface, destroying pollutants.

The challenge for scientists now is to make nanotechnology more affordable and producible on a large scale.

INNOVATIVE IDEA

In 2019, Anna Luísa Beserra from Brazil was one of seven young people to be presented with a "Young Champions of the Earth" award by the United Nations (UN). Anna Luísa had the idea of turning rain water into drinking water, using solar disinfection. She developed a rainwater harvesting system (see page 8) that purifies water using just sunlight and has a color-changing indicator to show when the water is ready. This low-cost device lasts up to 20 years and can be cleaned with soap and water.

Anna Luísa's technology uses the ultraviolet rays in sunlight to kill microbes in dirty water.

Anna Luísa Beserra

- **Age 15**, begins creating technology ideas for water treatment.
- **Age 17**, starts Safe Drinking Water for All, a company to develop her technology.
- **Age 21**, wins a Young Champions of the Earth award from UNEP (UN Environment Programme).

HARVESTING WATER

We have an almost constant supply of water on Earth, thanks to the water cycle. But the demand for water is rising, and we can't produce any more. To ensure there's enough to go around, we need to make use of all available sources and to store water for times of drought.

The water cycle is the continuous movement of water from the land and oceans to the sky and back again.

Water vapor condenses to form clouds.

Water falls back to Earth as rain or snow.

Water evaporates into water vapor.

Rivers flow towards the sea.

RAINFALL CAPTURE

Our drinking water usually comes from rivers, streams, lakes and underground reservoirs. But these sources make up just 40 percent of the rain that falls on Earth. We need to capture rainfall in other ways, too. In areas where water isn't always accessible, rain water can be collected from roofs, using simple gutters, downpipes and storage tanks. If the collecting surface is clean, only minimal treatment will be needed. More complex devices include filters, disinfectant treatment and pumped storage facilities.

In dry regions, rainwater harvesting is a cheap and simple way to bring freshwater supplies closer to home.

HUMID AIR

In humid environments, water can be extracted from the air, using technology similar to an air conditioner. When moisture-laden air passes over a chilled surface, it condenses because cool air can't hold as much water as warm air. The moisture can then be collected and filtered if necessary. However, this method uses a lot of electricity or solar power.

CONDENSATION CAPTURE

In areas without rainfall or humidity, there's still moisture in the air at certain times of day. Fog and dew catchers are mesh nets that catch water from the air. Taking inspiration from the needle-like leaves of redwood trees, scientists have recently designed fog "harps." These have vertical wires that increase the amount harvested from 1.2 to 3.5 cups per square foot (3 to 9 liters per square meter) a day.

By copying clever designs from nature (right), scientists have developed another water-condensing surface that pulls water from the air ten times faster than traditional methods.

Tiny bumps on the back of the desert beetle cause water droplets to form.

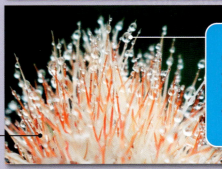

Cactus spines are shaped to direct water droplets towards the plant.

Water moves quickly on the slippery surface of the fly-catching pitcher plant.

DID YOU KNOW?

Spider webs are highly efficient at catching water from the air. As morning dew condenses on the spider silk, the droplets merge and get larger as they're pulled down by the force of gravity.

SMART CONTROLLERS

To look after our freshwater supplies, transporting water safely and efficiently is really important. In richer countries, most buildings are connected to a main's water supply and a wastewater drainage system. With a complex network of pipes in between, it's no surprise that problems arise.

Water companies keep maps of sewage pipes and mains' water supplies so that leaks can be found and fixed quickly.

DETECTING LEAKS

Around the world, about 1.5 billion cubic feet (45 million cubic meters) of water is lost each day through leaking pipes. Real-time leakage detection systems can help to address this problem. Sensors monitor the pipes 24 hours a day, recording sound and pressure levels. If changes are detected, water-stopping devices called valves can be shut remotely by a central computing system. Pipes can be fixed, and solutions put in place, often before the public become aware of a problem.

FARMING IRRIGATION

Most of our water supplies are used to help crops to grow and farm animals to thrive (see page 5). Irrigation systems direct water towards crops using channels, pipes and hoses, but they're not always efficient. Smart controllers can now be used on farms to collect data about weather conditions and soil moisture levels, so irrigation systems only target areas in need.

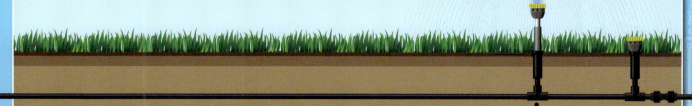

Studies have suggested that "precision irrigation" could help to reduce agricultural water usage by 25 percent.

SMART MONITORING

Over half of water use at home comes from baths, taps and toilet flushes. An average bath uses 21 gallons (80 liters) of water, a washing machine uses 13 gallons (50 liters) for an average wash and some toilets use up to 3.7 gallons (14 liters) per flush. Smart meters can help households to make informed choices about how much water they use (and how much money they spend). Studies have shown that water meters with real-time readings have reduced water consumption by 30 percent in some residential areas.

DID YOU KNOW?

The average person flushes the toilet over 1,500 times a year! A leaking toilet can waste over 185 gallons (700 liters) of water a day. This is the amount of water a household in India would use on average each day.

Dual flush toilets have a short or long flush option. They typically use 1–1.6 gallons (4–6 l) of water per flush, saving nearly 2.6 gallons (10 liters) a time.

FRESHWATER POLLUTION

Wastewater is fresh water that's become contaminated with human, agricultural or industrial waste. It can be harmful to health and can damage the delicate balance of Earth's ecosystems. The United Nations Water agency estimates that, globally, 80 percent of our wastewater flows back into the environment, without being treated and reused.

FARMING SOLUTIONS

Many farmers use chemical fertilizers and pesticides to increase their harvests. Rainwater can cause these chemicals to run into rivers and sink into the ground, poisoning ecosystems. Biological pest control is a more natural method. This involves introducing plants that deter pests (a method known as "companion planting"), or attracting insects that eat the pests. Drones can also now be used to identify pests so that chemical sprays are restricted to affected areas.

Ladybugs are an effective form of pest control. They eat an estimated 5,000 aphids in their lifetime!

INDUSTRIAL WASTE

Environmental regulations help to minimize the risk of industrial pollution, but greener industrial processes are an even better solution. For example, there have been concerns that fracking (a process of extracting natural oil and gas from the ground using high-pressurized liquids), pollutes water supplies and produces contaminated wastewater. A new proposed solution is water-free fracking, which uses a gelled fluid and requires an eighth of the quantity of liquid of traditional methods.

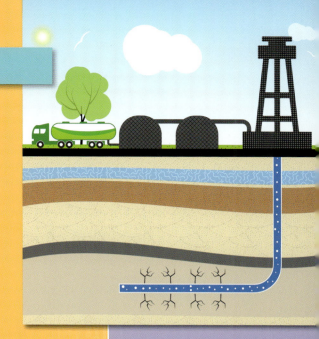

During a traditional fracking process, water sources can be polluted during the drilling stage or when wastewater comes back to the surface.

CLEANING UP

Wastewater treatment plants involve three main processes. Firstly, wastewater is filtered for large objects, and heavy solids settle at the bottom, while oil, grease and lighter solids float to the surface. Secondly, further filters are used, and bacteria breaks down some of the waste products. Finally, a disinfectant stage removes any harmful bacteria. Non-chemical, energy-saving treatments include the use of reed beds, sand filters and natural bacteria.

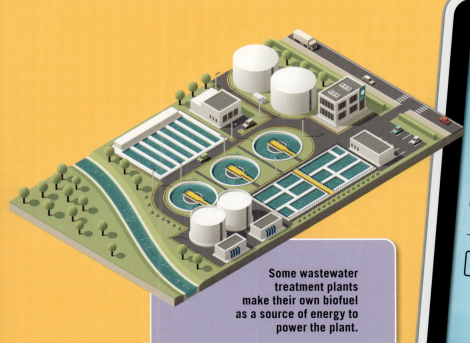

Some wastewater treatment plants make their own biofuel as a source of energy to power the plant.

Useful waste

- ✓ The "sludge" separated from wastewater can be used as a fuel or a type of fertilizer.
- ✓ Wastewater can also be used to grow algae for biofuel.
- ✓ Scientists have found ways to reclaim chemicals and minerals from wastewater to save on resources.

SALTWATER DESALINATION

About 96.5 percent of Earth's water is found in the oceans. But salt water isn't suitable for humans or many plants and animals to drink. Purified sea water is becoming an important water source in dry, coastal regions, however, when water is in short supply.

SALT EXTRACTION

The process of removing salt from sea water is called "desalination." There are two main types – thermal (where sea water is heated to produce water vapor) and membrane (where sea water is pushed through a series of filters). Thermal desal nation is more expensive and uses a lot of energy. It also produces more waste brine (dense salt water).

Desalination plants are useful in dry coastal areas, but if waste brine is pumped back into the ocean, it sinks to the bottom and harms marine life.

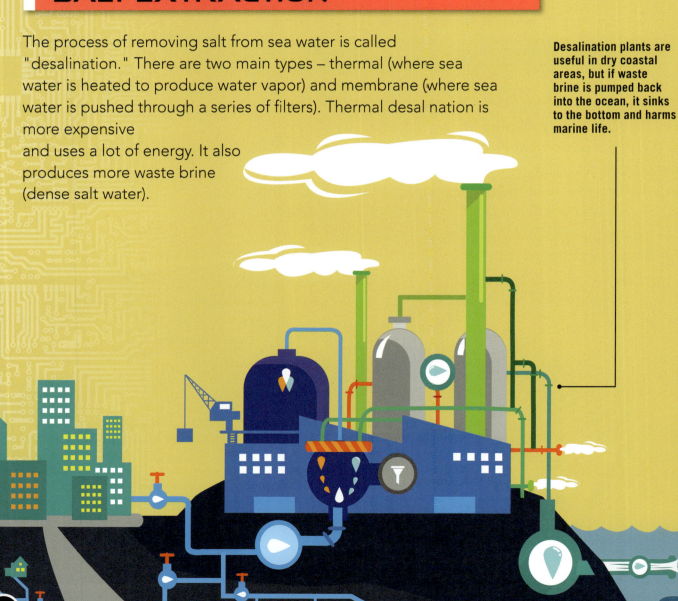

CUTTING COSTS

Scientists have developed solar-thermal desalination plants to help reduce energy costs. They have also found ways to turn waste brine into usable products. For example, salt (sodium chloride) can be split into sodium and chlorine ions which can then be used to make sodium hydroxide and hydrochloric acid. These can be used in industrial processes and to make goods, such as soap and paper.

This simple "solar still" uses heat from the Sun to form water vapor that condenses and runs into a collecting chamber.

NATURAL PROCESSES

Scientists are also turning to nature to find cheaper, less energy-intensive alternatives. They have studied the way that mangrove plants and saltwater fish filter out salts from sea water, for example. Although marine animals occasionally drink small amounts of sea water, they get the water they need from their food, and their bodies filter out the salt efficiently.

Mangrove plants filter out salt with their roots. They also push out salt into their leaves, so it's washed off by rain water or lost when old leaves drop off.

Salty solutions

✓ Desalination plants around the world produce around 100 billion litres of drinking water a day.

✓ It takes about 2.1 gallons (8 liters) of sea water to make 1 gallon (4 liters) of fresh water.

PLASTIC DEBRIS

Plastic waste is a hot topic right now. Scientists predict that at the current rate of pollution, there could be more plastic than fish in the sea by 2050. Plastic is harmful to marine life, puts food chains under threat and can disrupt the balance of Earth's ecosystems.

GREAT PACIFIC GARBAGE PATCH

The Great Pacific Garbage Patch is the world's largest collection of ocean plastic pollution – an estimated 620,000 square miles (1.6 million square km). Ocean currents have caused plastics to accumulate in this area and scientists are working to clean up the mess. A 1,970-foot (600-m) boom (floating barrier) is being used to gather and collect the debris, to be shipped to land and recycled. Rivers are also being cleaned up before they reach the sea.

The Great Pacific Garbage Patch covers an area three times the size of France!

CLEAN-UP OPERATIONS

In enclosed ocean areas, such as ports and harbors, the Seabin Project uses floating "bins" to suck up sea water, trapping litter, oil and fuel. "Waste sharks" have a vacuum-type design and collect floating waste and debris. Taking inspiration from the whale shark, the robot's large "mouth" can collect around 1,102 pounds (500 kilograms) of waste on a single charge.

The Seabin Project bins use pumps powered by renewable energy and can be used 24 hours a day, seven days a week.

MICROPLASTICS

Weathering and temperature changes at sea cause large plastic items to break down into smaller "microplastics." Instead of only floating on the surface, microplastics also sink deeper into the ocean and are difficult to remove. Scientists are using nanotechnology to help (see page 7). Tiny coil-shaped magnetic "nanosprings" can break down the microplastics into non-harmful compounds. The nanosprings can then be collected by magnets and used again.

Ocean waste

- More than 7.8 million tons of plastic end up in the oceans each year.
- Up to 35 percent of microplastics in the ocean come from synthetic clothes, that shed microfibers when washed. Exfoliating beads in some cosmetics and toothpastes are another source.
- Microplastics are so small, they can't be filtered by wastewater treatment plants. They can enter the food chain, causing harm to animals and humans.

OCEAN ACIDIFICATION

The effects of human activity have caused levels of carbon dioxide (CO_2) to increase in Earth's atmosphere. As well as causing climate change, some of this CO_2 has been absorbed by our oceans, causing them to become more acidic. Scientists are looking at ways to restore natural levels.

CARBON CAPTURE

The oceans absorb CO_2 in two ways. CO_2 dissolves in water to form carbonic acid. Animal and plant-like organisms (plankton and phytoplankton) also absorb CO_2. As they get bigger, some sink deeper into the ocean where carbon can be trapped for over 1,000 years. The effect on ecosystems is long-lasting. If ocean water becomes too acidic, some marine animals can't make strong shells, for example, and coral reefs are damaged.

dissolved CO_2

phytoplankton absorb CO_2 during photosynthesis

plankton use carbon as protective limestone covering

heavier organisms sink

dead organisms sink to the seabed

carbon also becomes trapped in the seabed

When oceans become more acidic, they are less efficient at absorbing CO_2, making climate change worse.

GEOENGINEERING

Some scientists have suggested adding large amounts of ground limestone to ocean water to help make the oceans less acidic. Limestone is alkaline (see diagram below) so it can help to balance the acidity of the water. This method has yet to be tested, however. Energy will be needed to mine and transport the limestone, and there are concerns this method may have unexpected consequences on marine ecosystems.

The pH scale measures how acidic or alkaline substances are. When acids and alkalis are mixed together, they neutralize.

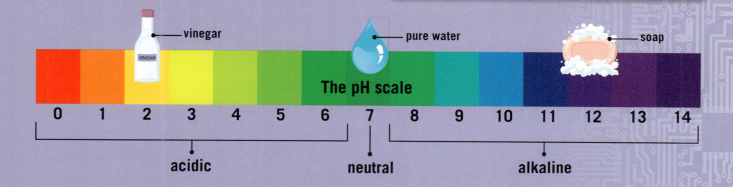

LOCAL SOLUTIONS

In smaller inshore areas, planting seaweed and other sea plants has helped to extract carbon dioxide from the air (through the process of photosynthesis) and keep it out of the sea water. The seaweed can then be harvested, dried and used as a fertilizer. Many people feel that reintroducing native sea plants is a more natural and safer solution than geoengineering.

Growing and harvesting seaweed in shallow waters helps to absorb CO_2 without making sea water more acidic.

Rising levels

- Every day, the ocean absorbs around 2.6 million tons of CO_2 from human activities.
- Each year, the ocean absorbs about a quarter of the CO_2 that our activities add to the atmosphere.
- Since the Industrial Revolution, the acidity of ocean waters has increased by 30 percent.

OIL SPILLS

Oil is a fossil fuel we use for transport, heating and to generate electricity. It is the remains of plants and animals that lived millions of years ago, found deep underground. Burning oil releases gases that cause Earth's temperatures to rise, and transporting it can bring a risk of pollution.

RISKY BUSINESS

When oil is extracted and transported around the world, there's potential for a leak or an oil spill. If huge amounts of oil are released into the environment, its quick spread has a devastating effect on wildlife, ocean habitats and coastal regions, and can contaminate food chains. Globally, approximately 1.4 million tons of oil are released into the sea each year.

DID YOU KNOW?

The world's largest oil spills have been oil tanker disasters, but spills from ships account for just 15 percent of oil entering the ocean each year. Pipelines are responsible for more than two-thirds of oil spilt on water or land, since they can contaminate rivers, streams and lakes.

NATURAL SOLUTIONS

For many years, oil spills were cleaned up using chemicals to break up the oil, floating booms to contain the spill, and non-biodegradable absorbent materials that soaked up the oil (but repelled water). Scientists have been looking at more eco-friendly solutions, such as the use of biodegradable straw, cotton and moss. For small oil spills, the water hyacinth plant has also been found to be particularly good at absorbing oil in a cost-effective way.

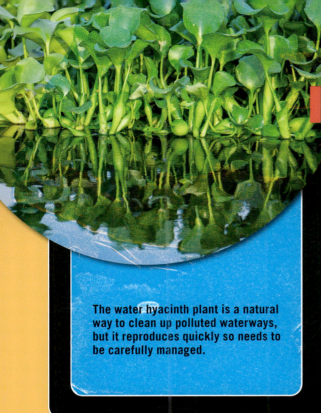

The water hyacinth plant is a natural way to clean up polluted waterways, but it reproduces quickly so needs to be carefully managed.

DRONES AT WORK

sea-cleaning drone

Specialized drones can also be used to survey the site of an oil spill. One idea under development is a "swarm" of drones that could be dropped by an aircraft. These drones have sensors to track the flow of an oil spill and release bacteria to help break down the oil. They use satellite navigation and a fuel cell (battery) powered by ocean water. The sea-cleaning drones also emit high-frequency sound waves to warn fish and other animals not to enter the polluted area. The challenge now is to secure funding to produce these drones on a large scale.

LIVING SHORELINES

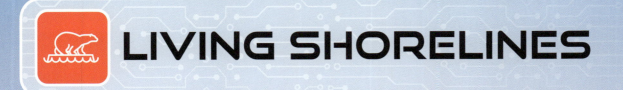

As climate change leads to rising temperatures on Earth, melting glaciers are causing sea level rises and more frequent flooding. This has a huge impact on those living in coastal regions and low-lying areas. Thankfully, green tech is finding ways to make vulnerable areas safer.

GROWING PROBLEM

Scientists predict that at the current rate of climate change, the homes of around 300 million people will be at risk of flooding at least once a year by 2050. Some islands and coastal cities could end up completely underwater, particularly in Bangladesh, India, China and Indonesia. In 2019, for example, the Indonesian government moved their capital city from Jakarta to the island of Borneo. Jakarta sits on swampy land and parts of the city are sinking, with almost half of it now below sea level.

Jakarta is the fastest-sinking city in the world. This is caused by a combination of rising sea levels and sinking land (due to the drilling of underwater wells).

STRONG DEFENCE?

For a long time, concrete walls were seen as a strong defence against advancing sea water. But to keep their strength, walls need to be maintained. When waves hit a wall, their energy is reflected, causing problems of erosion elsewhere. As an alternative solution, scientists have been looking at "living shorelines" to reduce the impact of flooding. Mangrove swamps, for example, trap mud in their sturdy roots, creating a natural barrier (see page 15).

The reflected energy in this wave will move down the coast and erode areas with weaker sea defences.

NATURAL BARRIERS

In calmer coastal regions, saltwater marshes can help to absorb rain water and trap sediment. They also dissipate (lessen) the energy of waves that erode the shoreline. Other natural barriers include ledges made of rocks, "logs" made of coconut fibers and bags of oyster shells. In badly hit areas, a mix of artificial and natural defences may be most appropriate.

DID YOU KNOW?

In the Arctic, the ice is 5 feet (1.5 meters) thinner on average each summer than it was 50 years ago. Although scientists are finding ways to defend coastal areas from flooding, they are also trying to address the root causes of glacial melting.

URBAN SOLUTIONS

The heavier rains brought by climate change are also causing inland areas to flood. The effects can be much worse in urban areas where flood water can't drain away through the soil. Impermeable surfaces such as roads and pavements cause the water to collect (or run into drains that may overflow).

ABSORBENT SURFACES

Permeable paving is one way to overcome this problem. One material developed by scientists (see right) has pores that absorb 1,056.7 gallons (4,000 liters) of water in the first minute, and about 158.5 gallons (600 liters) a minute thereafter! Drainage holes under the top layer help to collect water to be reused, or to be slowly drained into the surrounding soil. Permeable paving can be made from recycled materials, such as plastics, or waste products from cement or iron production.

- permeable top layer
- drainage holes drilled in previous surface
- permeable soil

PROS AND CONS

Permeable paving is a less slippery surface in winter because ice doesn't have a chance to form on it. With less water run-off, there's also less risk of water contamination from fuel leaks on road surfaces, and less erosion of surrounding soil. Scientists are looking at ways to make permeable paving less expensive and easier to maintain (the pores can become clogged, for example). Although a good solution for small roads, car parks, pavements and driveways, the material isn't suitable for motorways or airport runways yet, because the weight of heavy vehicles affects its permeability.

RAIN GARDENS

One cheaper alternative in urban areas is the use of rain gardens. These can be purpose-built flower beds underneath overhanging roofs, or large 'bowls' of dirt 108 to 323 square feet (10–30 square meters in diameter), filled with clay, sand and plants. The rain gardens are designed to collect run-off from houses and small buildings. The water sinks naturally into the soil or eventually evaporates (from the soil, or from plants that have absorbed the water).

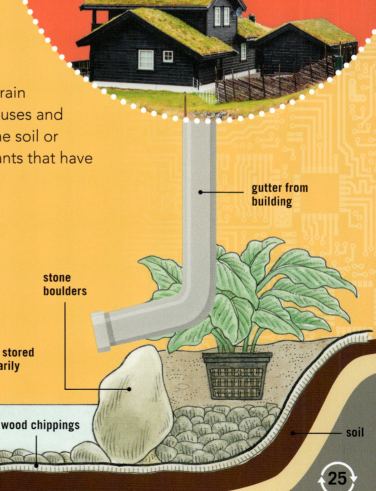

DID YOU KNOW?

Adding vegetation to roofs and walls helps to reduce the amount of water that runs off buildings. The plants trap and absorb the water, which is then absorbed by the air through evaporation.

SAVING WATER

While scientists are finding ways to collect and purify water, we can all help to reduce our water use and reuse our water supplies. We need water to drink, cook and wash, but water is also used to produce many of the things that we eat, use, buy or wear.

Food water footprints (gallons per pound)

Chocolate – 760
Beef – 1,857
Cheese – 6,000
Rice – 300
Asparagus – 2,150
Avocado – 260
Sugar – 180
Bread – 156
Banana – 103
Apple – 84

FAIR TRADE?

Every day, the average use of water per person on Earth is 1,004 gallons (3,800 liters). Over 90 percent of this comes from the "virtual water" of the products we buy. When richer countries import water-intensive goods, it can help the economy of the poorer nations exporting them. But this comes at a cost if water supplies there are used at the expense of basic drinking water and sanitation. It can be difficult to know the "water footprint" of the goods we buy (see left), but apps can now help us to make informed choices, using data from food labels or shopping receipts, for example.

The water footprint of a new car is up to 21,134 gallons (80,000 liters), while a new smartphone is around 3,170 gallons (12,000 liters).

Cotton grown in India uses 2,700 gallons per pound (22,500 liters per kilogram) of water.

THIRSTY CLOTHES

The clothes we buy are important, too. A pair of jeans, for example, use an average 800 gallons (3,000 liters) of water in their lifetime – about 49 percent to grow the cotton, about 6 percent in the manufacturing process, and 45 percent from regular washing. Companies are trying to improve these statistics. The Waterless range from Levi's®, for example, has reduced manufacturing water levels by 96 percent. The company has saved over 800,000 gallons (3 billion liters) of water (and recycled another 1.3 billion gallons [5 billion liters]) in the last decade and has pledged to make all its products from recycled cotton by 2025.

TAKING RESPONSIBILITY

We can all take care of the amount of water that we use at home (see page 11). Meanwhile, what we flush down the sink and the drains is important, too. Toxic products, such as chemicals and paints, need to be disposed of correctly. Grease and oil can also block pipes, causing water to back up and overflow.

Technology is finding new ways to reuse our waste materials. Paint, for example, can now be recycled with the help of an industrial vacuum cleaner that sucks the paint out of the tins quickly and efficiently.

BASIC SANITATION

In richer countries, sanitation facilities are often taken for granted. But studies show that two in five people worldwide don't have handwashing facilities at home and 2.5 billion people lack access to safe, sanitary toilets. Economic development is difficult without sustainable water supplies, so it's hard to break the cycle.

TOILET CHALLENGE

In 2012, the Gates Foundation challenged researchers to find a way to process human waste and turn it into useful resources, to support sanitation in poorer regions. First prize went to a team of scientists (below) from California, USA, whose solar-powered toilet produces fertilizer from waste products as well as hydrogen to power a fuel cell (battery) so the toilet can work in cloudy conditions. Other designs included the use of a worm that digests human waste and turns it into valuable garden compost, and a waterless toilet powered by the movement of closing the toilet lid.

The winning toilet design from the California Institute of Technology uses recycled water and doesn't need to be connected to a sewage pipe.

COVID-19

In 2020, the impact of coronavirus made handwashing a top priority around the world. Scientists sought to help people in poorer countries who lacked sanitation facilities. A London team working in Tanzania developed "single soap tabs" to reduce the need for soap to be shared. In Brazil, Anna-Luísa Beserra (see page 7) developed public handwashing stations that could harvest rain water from the roofs of bus stops and marketplaces, with a non-touch soap dispenser. In India, researchers developed a nozzle for plastic bottles to keep contact with taps to a minimum.

In 2020, studies showed that regular handwashing could reduce the spread of coronavirus by 36 percent. Innovative ideas needed to be found fast!

LAST WORD

World Water Day is held on March 22 each year. It's a time to reflect on a plentiful but precious resource and whether we're using it wisely. The world's water is constantly moving in a cycle, but each stage needs to be carefully managed. As the demand for water rises and climate change brings more challenging conditions, we need technology to support our actions more than ever.

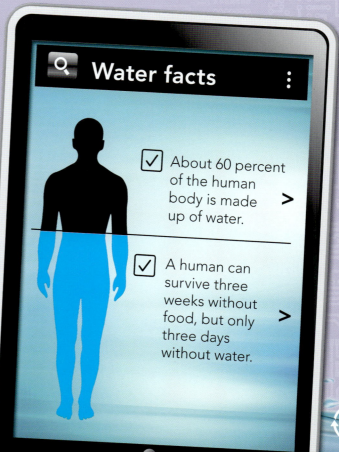

Water facts

✓ About 60 percent of the human body is made up of water.

✓ A human can survive three weeks without food, but only three days without water.

GLOSSARY

acidification when something becomes more acidic

biodegradable describes a material that breaks down naturally into the soil or water

biofuel fuel made from recent living matter, such as algae

climate change changes in long-term weather conditions and temperature patterns

contamination when something becomes polluted

disinfectant chemical liquid that destroys bacteria

drone unmanned flying device that can be controlled from a distance, or using sensors and satellite navigation

drought long period with little or no rain, leading to water shortages

ecosystem group of living things that interact with each other in an environment

erosion when materials are worn away by natural forces such as water and wind

evaporation the process of turning from a liquid into a gas

fertilizer chemical or natural substance added to soil to increase its fertility

glacier large mass of ice formed from compacted snow on mountains or in the polar regions

impermeable not allowing fluid to pass through

irrigation supply of water to land or crops to help them to grow

meltwater water that has melted from snow and ice, especially from a glacier

microplastics very small pieces of plastic (less than 0.2 inches [5 mm] in length) that can pollute the environment

pesticides substances used to destroy insects or organisms that damage crops

plankton (phytoplankton) microscopic (plant-like) organisms that float in the ocean

pollutants dirty, harmful or poisonous substances that pollute the air, soil or water

sediment naturally occurring materials, such as sand and small stones, that have broken down in the process of erosion

sewage waste water carried away from homes and workplaces, from drains and toilets

FURTHER INFORMATION

BOOKS

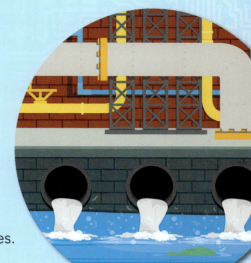

Source to Resource: Water: From Raindrop to Tap
by Michael Bright (Wayland)
Discover how the water we use reaches our homes.

Loos Save Lives: How sanitation and clean water help prevent poverty, disease and death
by Seren Boyd (Wayland)
The importance of sanitation and how one charity is changing lives.

Question It!: Water – Is there enough for everyone?
by Philip Steele (Wayland)
Find out how global conditions are threatening our water supplies.

VIDEOS

Water resources
youtube.com/watch?v=IDAj5T1ST7o
Learn how water is unevenly distributed around the globe and how we can make things more equal.

How we clean your drinking water
youtube.com/watch?v=HEhK5iVWoSg
Go behind the scenes of a water treatment works to see how our water goes from sky to tap.

The sewage treatment process
youtube.com/watch?v=8isr9nSDCK4
Take a journey through the sewage network!

INDEX

agriculture 5, 11, 12

animals 4, 14, 15, 17, 18, 20, 21

carbon dioxide (CO_2) 18, 19

climate change 5, 6, 18, 22, 23, 24, 29

desalination 14–15

diseases 4, 5, 29

drought 5, 8

flooding 5, 22, 23, 24–25

food 4, 15, 16, 17, 20, 26, 29

fresh water 4, 5, 8, 9, 10, 11, 12, 13, 15

Great Pacific Garbage Patch 16

harvesting water 5, 7, 8–9, 29

household use 5, 11, 27

industry 5, 12, 13, 15, 19, 27

leaks 5, 10, 11

permeable paving 24, 25

plants 4, 9, 12, 14, 15, 18, 19, 20, 21, 25

plastic 16–17, 24, 29

pollution 5, 7, 12–13, 16, 20, 21, 25, 27

purification 5, 6–7, 8, 14, 26

recycling 5, 12, 16, 24, 26, 27, 28

sanitation 11, 26, 28–29

sea water 5, 8, 14–15, 16–17, 18–19, 20, 21, 22–23

waste water 6, 10, 12, 13, 14, 15, 17

wastewater treatment 5, 6, 13, 17

water cycle 8

water footprint 26